THE YALE DRAMA SERIES

David Charles Horn Foundation

The Yale Drama Series is funded by the generous
support of the David Charles Horn Foundation, established
in 2003 by Francine Horn to honor the memory of her husband,
David. In keeping with David Horn's lifetime commitment
to the written word, the David Charles Horn Foundation
commemorates his aspirations and achievements by supporting
new initiatives in the literary and dramatic arts.

Still

JEN SILVERMAN

Foreword by Marsha Norman

Yale UNIVERSITY PRESS/NEW HAVEN & LONDON

Yale University Press books may be purchased in quantity for
educational, business, or promotional use. For information, please e-mail
sales.press@yale.edu (U.S. office) or sales@yaleup.co.uk (U.K. office).

Set in ITC Galliard and Sabon types by Integrated Publishing Solutions.
Printed in the United States of America.

Library of Congress Cataloging-in-Publication Data

Silverman, Jen.
Still / Jen Silverman ; foreword by Marsha Norman.
   pages   cm.—(The Yale drama series)
ISBN 978-0-300-20635-7 (pbk. : alk. paper)
I. Norman, Marsha. II. Title.
PS3619.I5477S86 2014
812'.6—dc23
2014005427

A catalogue record for this book is available from the British Library.
This paper meets the requirements of ANSI/NISO Z39.481-1992
(Permanence of Paper).
10 9 8 7 6 5 4 3 2 1

Contents

Foreword

The Yale Drama Series is unique among prizes given to emerging playwrights. It honors the memory of David C. Horn, a man who, though very successful, always wanted to have his own writing published. It is judged by a single judge, not a panel, not a committee, though the single judge always needs about eighteen readers to help screen the more than a thousand plays submitted each year. The winning playwright receives a check for $10,000, for which no future writing is expected; the money may be spent to travel or to pay rent, or it may be frittered away on books and food. This year's winner also received a reading at the Lincoln Center Theater's Claire Tow Theater, and this publication by the Yale University Press. There is no entry fee, a model more prizes should follow, and anyone can enter, provided the play has not received a professional production. Plays need not be sponsored or vetted, but are submitted by the playwrights themselves. Because of this generosity of spirit, many manuscripts that are entered are not plays at all, as you can imagine. But a great many of them are very, very good. And three or four are excellent. It has been my great honor to follow Edward Albee, Sir David Hare, and John Guare as a judge of this prize. I salute the fabulous Francine

Horn, whose labor of love this is, as well as her board of directors and supporters at Yale University.

I've read thousands of new plays in my time as a teacher and a reader for various prizes. The best ones are always about something large, and usually terrible, coming into someone's life, usually someone who is completely unprepared and consequently ill equipped to deal with it. These stories make the best plays because these terrible things are the ones that terrify us, that change us; they are the things we think we could not survive. We watch these plays as if they were happening to us. We watch for clues to how we might navigate the treacherous territory. We ask ourselves questions like "Why has this terrible thing happened?" and "Who is at fault here?" and "What must I do to ensure that this never happens to me?" Finally, depending on the skill of the writer and his or her knowledge of human life, the best plays always lead to the same point, a moment of recognition and relief. Sometimes there is redemption, sometimes there is forgiveness, but there is always a kind of peace that descends as the playwright brings order to the disorder, lifting the veil of shame and banishing the fear and violence that have ruled the stage.

Jen Silverman's play *Still* is such a play. It was discovered by an early reader, and heartily endorsed by the rest of the reader panel. When I read it, I knew immediately it was our winner. I have read other plays on the subject of a stillborn child, but none that live in such an existential plane, none as elegant in formal structure, none with language both surreal and trashy, none as funny, and none as moving. The refraction of the unbearable grief through the lives of all the characters, not just that of the mother, is the truly distinguishing characteristic of this play. The presence of the child himself is the mark of a master in the making.

We live with the dead child, Constantinople, for nearly a week as he searches for his mother, as his just born–just dead consciousness struggles to reconnect with someone he

knows only by the sound of her crying. That he first en-
counters a pregnant dominatrix and a guilt-stricken midwife
is no more surprising than his tall pale body and his operatic
vocabulary. His delights and fears, his experiments and ob-
servations are made all the more acute by the life that is
fading from him as we watch. He is the eternal wanderer,
caught between birth and death, fearing he will never know
love, only loss.

His mother, Morgan, is a portrait of grief, her own still-
ness also a powerful subject of the play. While the dominatrix
and the midwife flail about trying to find ways to exorcise
their guilt, she simply survives. And in this way she is still
present when her child returns and she can open her arms
to him at last. If he is the eternal wanderer, then she is the
eternal woman waiting for him to return home.

The play's classical antecedents are clear. Its contempo-
rary resonance is profound. This is no more a simple play
about a stillborn child than the *Odyssey* is a story about a
man who has angered the gods. This is a play about being
Lost, with Time running out. This play is about how we all
walk the path without a map, seeking help from strangers
and learning as much as we can, all the while preparing for
the end. That it is both graceful and eerie I will leave you to
discover for yourself. *Still* is a stunning achievement by a
young writer of great promise.

All writers have what we at Juilliard call their "stuff"—
that is, the topic that draws the best writing from them, the
situation that scares them the most, the subject that made
them want to write in the first place. If this subject, the ap-
pearance of the unbearable and unpredictable into the life
of an innocent who might as well be every member of the
audience, is Jen Silverman's "stuff," then we can look for-
ward to many more great plays from this year's Yale Drama
Series winner.

Marsha Norman

Still

Characters
(3F, 1M)

CONSTANTINOPLE   He is a giant newborn baby, dead. He
should be played by a fully grown, very tall
man. He is slippery, as unclothed as possible.
Unearthly, disturbing, and charming

MORGAN   Constantinople's mother, 41, fierce, grieving,
all angles

DOLORES   18, at odds with the world, from time to time
a dominatrix

ELENA   A young 30, a midwife, strongly principled,
scared

Time: Now

Places: A rundown hotel on the outskirts of a city
Morgan's basement

Playwright's Note: Actors must not cry in any moments *except*
those that are specifically indicated. Then (with the exception of
Constantinople's wailing, in Scene 9) they never give themselves
over to expressing grief fully—all crying is subtle and under-
stated. There is no moment in which these characters let themselves become sentimental. It is crucial that actors find and play
the dark humor and moments of real joy.

There is no intermission.

Scene One

A light on CONSTANTINOPLE.
He looks around. He looks at us.
He's delighted.
He has a plastic hospital bracelet around his ankle.

CONSTANTINOPLE   Wow.
Hi.
You're really beautiful.
I . . . That's great. How beautiful you are. That's . . . wow.
I'm not good with words yet. I'm learning them.
I learned a new one today. "Audacious." I overheard it. I
don't know how to use it yet.
(beat)
So. About me. I was born two days ago. I'm learning that
people may want to know this, about me, why I don't
know things yet.
(beat)
Things are just great here. Have you noticed? They're
great. Everything is so strange and great. I need more
words. I don't have enough words yet. Wow. You know?
Words are great.
(beat)
So that's me. I hope you like it. Being beautiful. Being
here. I hope you like it a lot. I was dead when I came out.
That was two days ago. Did I tell you that? I forget if I
told you that. I'm just having a look around. I just want
to see it—what I should have had.
(shift—darker)

Like you. I should have had you. Your faces. Your hands.
Your words.
(beat)
Don't feel bad or anything.
(listens for something, then stills as he hears it)
Oh. That's my mother. She's crying again.
She's very far away. I'm not sure where. I hear her in here.
(touches his stomach, where the umbilical cord was)
I don't know what she looks like. If you see her anywhere,
let me know.
I'd better go. I'm getting stiffer. I don't have much time.

CONSTANTINOPLE *leaves.*

Scene Two

A seedy hotel. Elegance faded, dilapidated, a grime that sort of shines.
DOLORES *sits on a pool table, cue in hand.*
She is dressed in hardcore dominatrix gear.
She plays pool against herself.

DOLORES   Your shot.
(she takes it, misses)
Ooh. Suckerrrr, my shot.
(she takes it, misses—as her opponent)
Pathetic.
(annoyed)
Fuck you.
(annoyed)
What did you say to me?

DOLORES *checks her watch.*
Then she moves the pool ball, sets up for a shot.
Then, spoiling for a fight with herself:

DOLORES   You can't do that!
—Watch me.
Put that back.
—Make me.
Girrrrl do *not* make me take out my combat boots.

A WOMAN *comes in, out of breath, in a hurry.*
She's wearing formal work clothes. She wears a carnival mask, and we can't see her face.

WOMAN   I'm sorry I'm late, I tried to call but I realized I don't have a number for you and—

DOLORES   You're five minutes overdue. You're five minutes ripe. You're a woman?

WOMAN   The traffic was crazy. I'm sorry.

DOLORES   You *are* a woman.

WOMAN   . . . Yes.

DOLORES   That's weird.
I usually get men.

WOMAN   I'm not a man.

DOLORES   Yeah, well, I'm aware of that. Now.
You gonna use that mask for Halloween?

WOMAN
(blurts out)
I'm a failure.

DOLORES   Yeah, I'm sure, but that wasn't what I asked. Halloween, yes or no?

WOMAN   I'm sorry?

DOLORES   Whatever, stop talking. Sit down.

The WOMAN *sits on the edge of the pool table nervously. She checks over her shoulder.*

WOMAN   Nobody I know would be here, right? I mean, this seems like the sort of place nobody I know would ever go, but then again *I'm* here, so . . .

DOLORES   Listen, we need to establish some rules right off the bat. I'm here to be mean to you. I'm good at that. And mean feels very honest to me, and I'm a very honest person, so it's great how my personality and my life goals line up. But I don't do clichés, because clichés are not honest, so I don't want to hear about how terrible you are or what a naughty girl you've been because blah blah blah WHATever NEXT. Are we clear?

Beat.

WOMAN   I've never done anything like this before.

DOLORES   Other house rules: If I get bored, I stop. If I get tired, I stop. If you don't suffer in a manner that I find enjoyable, I stop. I don't need to know your name, your occupation, or how you feel. Please for the love of God, don't talk about your feelings, this isn't a date. Which reminds me: you pay up front. Any questions?

WOMAN   This is all very new to me.

DOLORES   Cliff Notes version goes: pay up and shut up.

She holds out her hand.
The WOMAN *puts a roll of bills into it.*
DOLORES *counts them, then pockets them.*

WOMAN   It was a moment. A split-second. And then disaster. I look back on it again and again and I'm still not sure if it was my fault. But either way, I failed.

DOLORES   Look . . . you're not all that special. You know? Most of us aren't. So whatever you did is probably not all that special. Next to Hitler, you're . . . mediocre.

WOMAN   I try to tell myself that some failure is
inevitable. But I don't think it is. I think if you're good
at what you do—if you're prepared and educated and
precise—then you won't fail. But then I start asking
myself—where did I go wrong? And I don't know. I'm
prepared, I'm educated, I'm precise. I'm not boasting,
these are just facts. And I can't really sleep anymore. And I
can't eat. And the question shifts, you know. It becomes:
How can I ever atone? And I don't know that either. But
maybe you do.

DOLORES   Only the bourgeois upper middle class can
afford to worry about that shit. Do you want me to beat
you or not?

WOMAN   I don't know. Is that what we do here?

DOLORES   You're paying, you tell me what you want.
Slapping is OK. Hair-pulling. Some people like to be
kicked. Spanked. Thrashed.

WOMAN   Maybe if you just . . . shouted at me? A little?
There are certain phrases I remember from my childhood,
they were very upsetting to me. Maybe they'd be
appropriate in this context as well.

DOLORES   You want to be *yelled* at.

WOMAN   Well, yes, I thought that perhaps—

DOLORES   If you wanna be yelled at why don't you just
call your mother? People come here for hardcore shit. I'm
a hardcore person. You don't look like a hardcore person.

WOMAN   I'm not, I'm not a hardcore person. But I
was researching happiness on the internet, raw diets and

Buddhist mantras—and it all seemed just . . . very . . .
insincere.

DOLORES   Insincere?

WOMAN   Weak. Diluted. Redemption for beginners. I
need advanced redemption. And then I saw your website.
And it seemed like a very extreme solution, true, but I'm
in a very extreme place right now.
(DOLORES *looks ill.*)
What's wrong?

DOLORES *throws up.*
The WOMAN *is nervous but she's good at this kind of thing; she
holds* DOLORES'S *hair back gently.* DOLORES *lets her briefly,
then sits up, already better, and shoves her away.*

WOMAN   Did I say something?

DOLORES   Don't flatter yourself, it's just food
poisoning.

WOMAN   What did you eat?

DOLORES   Or allergies.

WOMAN   Those are pretty intense allergies.

DOLORES   I'm *allergic* to *food poisoning.*
(she straightens, already back to business)
You should go.

WOMAN   Go?

DOLORES   Reschedule.

WOMAN   I didn't mean to upset you.

DOLORES   You look stupid in that mask.

The WOMAN *takes off her mask. It is* ELENA.
She leaves. DOLORES *sits on the pool table. She rubs her stomach.*

DOLORES
(to her stomach)
Fuck.

Scene Three

CONSTANTINOPLE   Wow. Hello. I just, the weirdest
thing just happened. I was walking and then my hands
were wet. And then my head was wet. And then
everything was wet! The—
(points up, to the sky)
Up there was wet. And the wet was falling, so down here
was wet. It was—
(struggling)
Wow.
So that happened.
HardCORE.
(delighted)
Oh I learned that one too. It's new. There were two
(gestures: male teenagers, chains and tattoos)
big. people. and they were all FuckYou
NoFuckYouMuhfucka and then they said: hardCORE.
(beat, tries the word)
Muhfucka.
(out to the audience)
Can you tell me what that means?
(beat)
Maybe later.
(beat)
My mother played me The Ramones. She played The
Grateful Dead. She played me recordings of the collected
calls of all the insects in the Northern Hemisphere, and
parts of the Southern Hemisphere as well. She likes insects.
She read me the dictionary. I learned a lot of words that

way but not all of them. Some of them got stuck in her throat before they reached me. Sometimes she didn't enunciate.
(listens)
She's not crying today.
I'd like to find her. When she starts crying, I walk and walk. My joints are getting stiffer. Sometimes I have to stop. I wait for her voice to get closer but it hasn't yet.
(listens)
Oh! There she goes.

He walks off.

Scene Four

MORGAN'S *house. The basement.*
A single window, high up, at ground level.
Dirt floor. Dim.
MORGAN, *despondent, in her bathrobe, sits on the floor.* ELENA
sits with her.

MORGAN   I did everything right.

ELENA   I know.

MORGAN   The things I ate. The things I didn't eat. The
things I drank or didn't drink. Nine months without wine.
Water aerobics. Everything you told me to do. Why is it
my fault?

ELENA   It's not your—

MORGAN   Why do I feel like it's my fault?
(cuts ELENA *off)*
Don't answer that.
I don't want to see anybody. Ever again.

ELENA   OK.

MORGAN   I just want to sit here. Moss will grow. Up
over my face. Like a burka of moss. Moss will grow over
the basement. Over the door. Over the house. I'll just sit
here forever in a subterranean pocket of moss. It will get

hard to breathe and everything will be very green but at least nobody will drop by with casseroles.

ELENA   Morgan . . .

MORGAN   What.

ELENA   The casseroles are people being nice. It's a midwestern thing I guess.

MORGAN   Fuck nice. I don't feel nice. I don't want anybody else to feel nice. I want everybody to be miserable. More miserable than me. I know I'm competitive, but this time I want everybody else to win.
(beat)
Don't you have somewhere to be?

ELENA   Do you want me to go?

MORGAN   I didn't say that, I just asked if you had somewhere to be.
Don't answer that.
I feel crazy. I'm sorry.

ELENA   Do you want some casserole?

MORGAN   Which kind?

ELENA   The one with the pink stuff in it.

MORGAN   Bacon, that's bacon.

ELENA   No, the gray stuff is bacon.

MORGAN   The pink stuff is also bacon.

Beat.

ELENA   Is that a yes?

MORGAN   Yeah, whatever, no, OK.

ELENA *gets* MORGAN *casserole.*
MORGAN *holds it throughout but doesn't eat.*

ELENA   Maybe we could go eat upstairs.
In the dining room. Or the kitchen. Or the living room.
Or you could take a hot shower? Change your clothes?

MORGAN   They didn't want to see the photos. I said:
Wanna see the photos? But none of them did.

ELENA   I know.

MORGAN   He was beautiful.

ELENA   I know.

MORGAN   He was dead but he was beautiful.
(beat)
They think it's my fault.

ELENA   Nobody—

MORGAN   *Everybody*, Elena, *everybody*—and they think
if I'd had him in a hospital he would have been fine—this
whole crazy thing of a homebirth, they're thinking, it
sounds Greenpeace and hippie and Little House on the
Prairie and in the end her baby is dead. That's what
they're thinking. And if they're not thinking it's *my*
fault, then they're thinking it's yours. The midwife,
after all.

A beat. This hits hard.

ELENA   It's neither of our faults. We took every
precaution. Every care. It was a safe and healthy delivery—

MORGAN   Until it wasn't.

Beat.

ELENA   Do you think it's my fault?

Beat.

MORGAN   I didn't say that.

ELENA   There was nothing Little House on the Prairie
about any of this, Morgan, and you know that. We
followed the designated standard of care, I've delivered
hundreds of babies without incident and this one time—

MORGAN   There was incident.

Beat.

ELENA   Yes.

MORGAN   Say it.
(beat)
"There was incident." Say it.
(beat)
Just say it!

ELENA   "There was incident!"
Morgan, this isn't easy for me either. I've never lost a child
before. Never.

MORGAN   Well me neither, Elena, I've never lost a child
either.

(beat)
I would have wanted to see the photos. If it was somebody else's baby. I would've wanted to see. Wouldn't you?

ELENA   I would. I would have too.

She touches MORGAN's *hand.*
MORGAN *lets her.*

MORGAN   Where do you think he is?

ELENA   They're preparing him.

MORGAN   He should be here. With me. They can't prepare him for anything I wouldn't prepare him for better.

ELENA
(gently)
They're preparing him to be buried.

MORGAN   I don't care.
A coin on his tongue. Coins on his eyes. Snacks for the road.
That's what I would have done.
I want to see him. When can I see him?

ELENA   Let me get you some more casserole.

MORGAN   I WANT MY FUCKING SON.
(beat)
I never got to hold him.
I was scared when they said, "Do you want to hold him?"
I was scared of him.
I wish I'd held him.

ELENA   I'm sorry.

MORGAN
(turning away, cutting)
It's not *your* fault.

Scene Five

In the dilapidated hotel.
DOLORES, *sprawled on the pool table.*
She tells dead baby jokes to her stomach.

DOLORES   What do you call a dead baby in a swimming pool?
(beat)
Bob.
(beat)
What do you call a dead baby on a beach?
(beat)
Sandy.
(beat)
What do you call a limbless dead baby in a pile of leaves?
(beat)
Russel.
(beat)
What's funnier than a dead baby?
(beat)
A dead baby in a clown costume!
(to her stomach)
I'm not raising you, I'm killing you. But if I were raising
you, I'd raise you with a killer sense of humor. That means
you'd massacre thousands while you laughed.
(beat)
We'd get along. I'd read your tea leaves. You'd learn tarot.
We'd both learn to tango. We'd tango around the room
of a garret somewhere in Paris. High above the city. You

would plan your latest crimes and you would run them all
past me. I would give them the A-OK and then you would
carry them out. You'd wear spurs. I'd have a top hat. We'd
escape into the Wild West, once we got sick of Paris. You'd
be a crack-shot sharpshooter. I'd be an alcoholic. It would
be awesome. Wouldn't it be awesome?
(beat)
Too bad I'm not raising you.
(beat)
The quality of humanity is going down. There have been
studies.

CONSTANTINOPLE *appears in the doorway.*
He watches her with interest.

DOLORES   Who the fuck are you, room service?

CONSTANTINOPLE   I'm Constantinople.

DOLORES   Excellent, I'm Darfur. Move along, cupcake.

CONSTANTINOPLE   What are you doing?

DOLORES   Talking to myself. Are you retarded?

CONSTANTINOPLE   No, I'm Constantinople.
Have you seen my mother?

DOLORES *looks him up and down.*

DOLORES   You look weird.

CONSTANTINOPLE   You look sad.

DOLORES   Fuck you, I'm Comedy Central. Life's a
dream. Row row row your Sound of Music. You seriously
look weird.

CONSTANTINOPLE   Well, I'm young.

DOLORES   So am I and I know how to dress myself.
No excuse.

CONSTANTINOPLE   I died two days ago.

DOLORES   And I have plans to kill myself next week.
Get into the Waaaambulance, this pity party got shut
down.

CONSTANTINOPLE   I was born two days ago.

DOLORES   Oh.

Beat.

CONSTANTINOPLE   You're very hard to understand.
Is that normal?

DOLORES   Are you a boy or a girl?

CONSTANTINOPLE   I'm a boy.

DOLORES   Where's your Mom?

CONSTANTINOPLE   She's not here?

DOLORES   No, I don't think so. No.

CONSTANTINOPLE   When she stops crying, I get
confused.

DOLORES   I don't think you're old enough to be here.

CONSTANTINOPLE   I got lost. I walked and walked
and then she stopped crying and I was lost. But then I

smelled her. And I followed it here. But now you're here and you don't smell like my mother at all. I need her to start crying again.

DOLORES   Sounds like she cries a lot.

CONSTANTINOPLE   She cries until she falls asleep. I can tell when she cries in her sleep because it's muffled.

DOLORES   I don't cry.

CONSTANTINOPLE   Not ever?

DOLORES   Not ever.

CONSTANTINOPLE   What do you do?

DOLORES   I hit people mostly. If I start feeling emotional.

CONSTANTINOPLE   Does it help?

DOLORES   Well, I'm feeling emotional. Come here.

CONSTANTINOPLE *approaches. She punches him in the arm.*

CONSTANTINOPLE
(surprised)
Ow.

DOLORES   And now I feel better.

CONSTANTINOPLE   Wow.

DOLORES   What?

CONSTANTINOPLE   Do that again.

DOLORES   Freak.

CONSTANTINOPLE   It felt . . . It felt . . . It felt . . .
Wow.

DOLORES   You like that shit?

CONSTANTINOPLE   HardCORE.

DOLORES
(sizes him up—with some interest)
Yeah OK.
(punches him in the arm again)

CONSTANTINOPLE   Wowww!

She punches him again, harder.

CONSTANTINOPLE   Audacious!
(she goes to punch him again, he pulls away)
That's enough.

DOLORES   Pussy.

CONSTANTINOPLE   Can I do it to you?

DOLORES   No.

CONSTANTINOPLE   Pussy.

DOLORES   I'm *not* a pussy, I will fuck you up.

CONSTANTINOPLE   What's that one?

DOLORES   Huh?

CONSTANTINOPLE   "Fuck." I hear it a lot.

DOLORES
(*stares at him, then*)
Wow.

CONSTANTINOPLE   Wow?

DOLORES   It's like wow, only better.

Beat.

CONSTANTINOPLE   Is this your place of residence?

DOLORES   Yes. No. Now it is.
I don't know. I ran away. I became a dominatrix. Now I'm
insane.

CONSTANTINOPLE
(*impressed*)
Fuck.

DOLORES   Yeah, fuck. You ever met a crazy woman
before?

CONSTANTINOPLE   No I don't think so.

DOLORES   Oh honey. We're a dime a dozen. Common
as lice. But god*damn* can we make a scene.
You gonna sit or what?
(CONSTANTINOPLE *perches on the edge of the pool table*)
So I'm crazy and you're dead. That's the first thing that's
made sense in like eighteen years. What's it like?

CONSTANTINOPLE   Being dead?
Oh, I don't know. Everything is very strange. I don't
understand any of it. I feel very confused.

DOLORES   That sounds pretty much the same as being alive.

CONSTANTINOPLE   Everything is very beautiful.

DOLORES   And there's the big difference.
You're the strangest person I've ever met.

CONSTANTINOPLE   I'm sorry.

DOLORES   That's OK.
I think that's definitely OK.
You wanna see my room?

CONSTANTINOPLE   You have a room?

DOLORES   It's a garret, it's filthy, there's cockroaches, you'll love it. Come on.
(she gets off the table, CONSTANTINOPLE *follows; at the door—)*
Don't get any funny ideas. Just because I'm rude doesn't mean I'm a slut.

CONSTANTINOPLE   "Slut"?

DOLORES   I'll explain later.

She leads CONSTANTINOPLE *out of the room.*

Scene Six

MORGAN *and* ELENA. *In the basement.*
ELENA, *on the phone, on hold.*
MORGAN *is pacing and* ELENA *is trying to get her to sit down.*

MORGAN   What do they mean they *lost* him.

ELENA   Morgan—

MORGAN   How do you LOSE a dead CHILD?

ELENA   It's a misunderstanding, I'll sort it out. But—

MORGAN   You're on HOLD.

ELENA   Please—

MORGAN   You are not SORTING things OUT. You are on HOLD. Witness the unifying metaphor for human LIFE.

ELENA   Please sit down.

MORGAN   Give me that.
(she snatches the phone)
LISTEN, FUCK YOUR ELEVATOR MOZART, I WANT A GODDAMN HUMAN BE— Hello? Hello. I am the MOTHER of the CHILD you MISPLACED. He may be dead but I am still his mother and he is still my

child and where the fuck is he, I am an American citizen
and I will sue you so hard you piss blood.
(listens—then, with dignity:)
I don't care if you're sorry. I want to see my son. You're
going to stick him in the earth and then it will be winter
and the ground will be hard and he won't even be able
to hear me through the snow and the ice and that is not
FAIR. It is not FAIR that there will be twelve feet of snow
and ice between us. So I want you to do something to
make this FAIR. What do you think about that?
(listens)
Well you better do it stat.
(hangs up)
They said they'll find him.

ELENA
(faintly)
That's wonderful.

MORGAN   Being divorced with a midwife is almost
exactly like being married with a husband. I still have to
do everything around here.

Beat.

ELENA   Would you like some casserole?

MORGAN   No.

Beat.

ELENA   Morgan, I haven't wanted to burden you, but
I—there's been something that I—

MORGAN   You were waiting for him to show up. You
know? You were ready for when he showed up, so you

could be useful. But for me . . . he'd already showed up.
He was right here.
(hand on her stomach)
I miss him right here. Everything is too flat right now.
Inside me and around me. I need it to be not-flat. That's
what I need.

ELENA   I'll help. I can help.

MORGAN   I don't think so.
(beat)
I'm sorry.
I'm not an emotional person.
These are not emotions, per se.
I prefer to think of them as—natural disasters.
(beat)
You were going to tell me something.

ELENA   We can talk about it later.

MORGAN   You didn't want to burden me but blah blah
blah. Yes? Burden me now.

ELENA   I didn't know you were listening.

MORGAN   I always listen, I just ignore. Years as a
college professor taught me that. It would have been a
good skill to have as a mother, too, I think. Anyway.
Go on.

Beat.

ELENA   The Board of Nursing is doing an inquest.

MORGAN   I'm sorry?

ELENA   An examination. They'll be calling to talk to you.

MORGAN   Will they.

ELENA   They say they want to make sure that the proper standard of care wasn't violated.

MORGAN   They want somebody to blame?

ELENA   No, no, nothing like—

MORGAN   They want to blame you.

Beat between them.

ELENA   They—yes. They would like to know that babies cannot be delivered properly outside of a hospital. Outside of a man's capable hands. Outside.

MORGAN   What does this inquest look like?

ELENA   They're going to ask you questions. About what happened during the labor, at which point I decided you needed transport to the hospital. They're trying to understand if my judgment was within the standard of care. What you tell them—and what they decide—will be important. I don't have to tell you that. For me, yes, but not just for me. For my clients. For women like you.

Beat.

MORGAN   Did you practice that in front of the mirror a few times?

ELENA   Morgan—

MORGAN   You practiced it. Come on. Women like me? Tragedy is alienating. These days as far as I'm concerned there's nobody like me.

ELENA
(quiet)
I don't deserve to lose my license.

A beat. MORGAN *sizes her up.*

MORGAN
(not angry; dead serious now)
You have that much faith?

ELENA   In what?

MORGAN   In your abilities. In your—I don't know.
Judgment. You don't doubt for one second that you could
have made a mistake?
(studying her—then with certainty)
You doubt. You have doubts.
(beat, ELENA *looks away)*
But I wanted Constantinople to come into the world his
way. My way. At home. So then maybe it's my fault again.

ELENA
(in a rush)
I've wanted my whole life to be good at this. And I don't
know if I made a mistake, I wish I knew, I wish I could
say, "This is what I did wrong." It's the not knowing that
makes me question everything—which was the second in
which I failed? Because the only fact I have, Morgan, is
that somehow, somewhere, I'm guilty of failure. And the
weight is unlike any other.

A beat.

MORGAN   I despise weak women. I despise weak
anyone, but I especially despise weak women. Ones who
are overcome by sentiment. Ones who, in the face of

tragedy, do not have the courage and the self-worth to say:
I did my best. I tried my hardest. This is not my fault.
If I were your mother, I'd be so proud of you.

ELENA You—?
Thank you.

MORGAN
(*gently*)
You're welcome. Now get out of my house.

ELENA Morgan—?

MORGAN Please.
(*Half-beat.* ELENA *leaves. To herself:*)
I did my best. This is not my fault.
I did my best.
I did.
(ELENA *returns. She's carrying a giant pumpkin.*)
You're still here.

ELENA I'm going. But I just—I knew you wouldn't
want a casserole. So this is what I have.

MORGAN A . . . pumpkin?

ELENA I stole it from your neighbor's porch.

MORGAN What am I supposed to do with that?

ELENA It isn't flat.

Beat.
MORGAN *looks at* ELENA.
She looks at the pumpkin.
ELENA *has a point. It is not, in fact, flat.*

ELENA *sets the giant pumpkin in her lap.*
MORGAN *holds it.*
A beat.
She runs her fingers over it.
A beat.
She puts her ear to it.
As she does these things:

ELENA   I know he was your son, not mine. But I wake
up in the morning and he's dead and I go to sleep and
he's dead and I pulled him out into the world dead, and
it eats at me and eats at me and you're the only person in
the world who understands right now. How different the
world looks. Without him in it. And your different world
and my different world are maybe not the same different
world. But all I can say is that—I would have loved your
little boy. I would have loved seeing him grow up and
knowing that I invited him into the world and coming to
his birthday parties. I wish that could have happened. And
now I'll go.

Beat.

MORGAN   You know this pumpkin is dead?

ELENA   What?

MORGAN   It's not plugged into the earth anymore.
The vines are cut. It doesn't grow.
It's dead, Elena.

ELENA   Oh.

MORGAN
(pulling the pumpkin against her)

I'll love it anyway.
For the time being.

A beat. ELENA *goes.*
MORGAN *cradles the pumpkin.*
She hums it a lullaby.

Scene Seven

The dilapidated hotel.
DOLORES *and* CONSTANTINOPLE *sit.*
DOLORES *has a bottle of black nail paint. She paints her fingernails.*

DOLORES
(rapid-fire)
I meant to tell William that I was preggo and then I just
stabbed him. You know? It happens like that sometimes,
your words fail you and something else asserts itself. I
stabbed him in the neck with a fork. I meant to aim for the
heart, it seemed more symbolic at the time. I was upset, I
was shaky, I misaimed, I said YOU DON'T EXPECT ME
TO DEDICATE MY LIFE TO YOUR MISTAKE, DO
YOU? and then I stabbed him in the neck. I feel like I've
been talking a lot. Tell me about you.

CONSTANTINOPLE   What happened when you
stabbed him?

DOLORES   He bled of course, it was very unsatisfying,
probably for both of us. Probably if I were to do it again
I'd forgo symbolism and just aim for what would hurt the
most. Testicles are a good bet, it would be like putting a
fork into a poached egg.

CONSTANTINOPLE   What's a poached egg?

DOLORES   I thought if William bore the marks of my
fork in his testicles, he'd be forced to reevaluate the moral
code by which he lives his life. I believed he might ask
himself—or at least the internet—a whole new set of
questions, even if they started: HOW DOES ONE
GENTLY AND CAREFULLY REMOVE A FORK
FROM A TESTICLE and ended with WHAT DOES
ONE DO WITH JUST ONE BALL?

CONSTANTINOPLE   Did he—um—reevaluate his
moral code?

DOLORES   He doesn't return my calls now. How did
you get here anyway?

CONSTANTINOPLE   I hitchhiked from the morgue.

DOLORES   How was that? Oh wait, let me guess—

DOLORES & CONSTANTINOPLE   —Beautiful.

DOLORES   Fuckin hippie.
(re: nail paint)
I'll do you.

CONSTANTINOPLE   You—?

DOLORES   Unless, like, you're too much of a man for
this or some shit.

CONSTANTINOPLE
(genuinely asking)
I don't know. I'm three days old now. Is that too much of
a man?

DOLORES   No not yet.
Come here. Closer.
I'm not gonna get all crazy on you.

CONSTANTINOPLE *scoots closer on the bed.*
DOLORES *grabs his foot, pulls it over her lap.*

CONSTANTINOPLE   OH.

DOLORES   What?

CONSTANTINOPLE   That feels—

DOLORES   No hippie adjectives.

CONSTANTINOPLE   I've never touched anyone before.

DOLORES   Wait, really?

CONSTANTINOPLE   Not like this. Outside-to-outside.
Your outside feels . . . weird.

DOLORES   Do you like it?

CONSTANTINOPLE   Yes, I think so. It's—there's a
moment—when the up-there gets wet—

DOLORES   Sky.

CONSTANTINOPLE   —and the down-here gets wet—

DOLORES   Earth.

CONSTANTINOPLE   —and those things slide against
each other.
That's what it feels like.

DOLORES *can't help smiling.*

DOLORES   Hold still.
(she starts to paint his toenails black)
This isn't going to get all shady. If you were wondering.
I don't sleep with men. Not often. Except William, and
that was a mistake, I thought he was a tranny and then he
wasn't.

CONSTANTINOPLE   A what?

DOLORES   Sometimes I make mistakes, I don't usually
remember their names, but William—I fucked him by
mistake and then I remembered it by mistake. He said he
was going to change his name to Wilhelmina, that kind
of turned me on. He's still William though, I checked on
Facebook. Tell me your name again.

CONSTANTINOPLE   Constantinople.

DOLORES   Yeah, I wouldn't sleep with you, even if you
were older. That's too nice of a name.

CONSTANTINOPLE   Thank you.

DOLORES   I don't really like people that much but
you're OK.

CONSTANTINOPLE   I think you're Wow.

DOLORES
(touched)
Really?

CONSTANTINOPLE *nods vigorously.*

DOLORES
(trying to man up)
That's stupid. How come?

CONSTANTINOPLE   I've never met anybody like you
before.

DOLORES   That's not saying much, you've got like sixty
hours under your belt and you're not even alive. You gotta
try harder to flatter a lady.

CONSTANTINOPLE   I think you're very pretty.

DOLORES   How would you know?

CONSTANTINOPLE   You look like words I haven't
learned yet.

DOLORES
(soft)
You're not at all like me. That's probably why I think
you're OK.
You can paint my fingernails when I'm done.

CONSTANTINOPLE   I don't know how.

DOLORES   Just watch what I'm doing, you can do that.
But only black, though, that's the only color I have, I'm a
punk rock bitch, not a *girl*.
(beat)
I hate girls. If I thought I was giving birth to one, I'd just
fucking kill myself right now.

CONSTANTINOPLE   I like girls.

DOLORES   You would.
(beat)

I mean, I'm not saying men are good or nice or great, they're liars and losers and motherfuckers mostly but I *like* the lying and losing and motherfuckery because I can understand it. Girls have too much hope. This is why I thought you were a girl at first—sorry about that—you just seemed so—polite—and politeness is, after all, nothing but the hope that politeness will be returned. I don't usually talk this much. Except to myself. OK, one foot done, what do you think?

CONSTANTINOPLE   It's very . . . black.

DOLORES   Looks good on you. Give me the other one.
(pulls the other foot into her lap and then stops)
You know you got jewelry?

CONSTANTINOPLE   Jewelry?

DOLORES   Here.
(takes out a switchblade, cuts the hospital bracelet around his ankle)

CONSTANTINOPLE   Give me that!

DOLORES   Easy, killer.
(reading)
Your mother's name is Morgan.

CONSTANTINOPLE
(trying it out)
"Morgan"?

DOLORES   That's what it says.
(gives him the bracelet)
You're carrying her name around on you and you don't even know it?

CONSTANTINOPLE
(smells it)
I can't read.
It smells like her.
Does it say where she is?

DOLORES   Where she is?

CONSTANTINOPLE   So I can talk to her.

DOLORES   Talk to her?

CONSTANTINOPLE   See her.

DOLORES   See her?

CONSTANTINOPLE   What?

DOLORES   I don't know.

CONSTANTINOPLE   No, what.

DOLORES   "See her"—I don't know.

CONSTANTINOPLE   What, though.

DOLORES   People are kind of weird. About that. About
things like that. Maybe she wouldn't want you to just—
show up—and see her. You know?

CONSTANTINOPLE   So maybe I could send her a
letter.

DOLORES   A letter.

CONSTANTINOPLE   I could say Wow to her.

DOLORES   "Hello." Not "Wow." In these
circumstances.

CONSTANTINOPLE   That's what I meant.

Beat. DOLORES *doesn't look at him.*

DOLORES   I mean. You could. But like. Maybe,
whatever. You know?

CONSTANTINOPLE   No I don't know.

DOLORES   I mean, a letter, maybe she doesn't want a
letter. You're dead, right? So maybe she probably would
rather you don't write to her. Dead people don't write
letters that often, it's kind of uncommon. You know?
(beat)
What.

CONSTANTINOPLE   *I* would want a letter from *her.*

DOLORES   She's not dead.

CONSTANTINOPLE   Even if she were. I would want
her to tell me things.
(with increasing intensity)
I would want her to tell me the things she told me when I
was inside that I couldn't hear properly. I think they were
important and I'd want to hear them again, hear them
better. I'd want her to tell me about my name. How nice
it is and how she picked it and how much she enjoyed
saying it.
(faster and faster)
And about the music she played for me, if she listens to
that now and thinks about me and if she set things aside
for me, books or places or stories she's only ever wanted to

tell one person in the universe and that person is me, I'd want her to tell me why she didn't do it why she didn't do it why she didn't DO it RIGHT so that I could be there, outside, there with HER and not HERE.

Beat.

DOLORES
(small, hurt)
It isn't so bad here.

CONSTANTINOPLE
(recovering from emotion)
No.

DOLORES   With me. It isn't bad.

CONSTANTINOPLE   No, it isn't bad.

DOLORES   Believe it or not, there are worse places to be. Outside of here. Away from me.

CONSTANTINOPLE   I didn't mean it that way.
(DOLORES *turns away)*
I didn't, though.
Dolores?
I just wanted to see her.

DOLORES
(muffled)
That makes me sad.

CONSTANTINOPLE   Why?

DOLORES   I've started to want you to be here. With me. It makes me feel . . . not lonely.

CONSTANTINOPLE   You could help me write the letter. You could say something too.

DOLORES   What would *I* say to your mother?

CONSTANTINOPLE   I don't know. You've been around a lot longer than me. You could say something comforting.

DOLORES   You don't sound like you want to be comforting, you sound pissed off.

CONSTANTINOPLE   Pissed off?

DOLORES   Angry. Mad. ARRRRRGH. Like that.

CONSTANTINOPLE   OH.
(*"listens" to his feelings, wide-eyed*)
Is that what this is?

DOLORES   Yeah, I think so, yeah.

CONSTANTINOPLE   Wow. I don't know how to be "pissed off."
(*beat*)
Dolores?
Don't be sad.
(*beat*)

DOLORES   Do my toenails.
(CONSTANTINOPLE *learns how to paint her toenails black as she composes a letter.*)
How does this sound: "Dear Mother. I am dead."

CONSTANTINOPLE   "Mother?"

DOLORES   What.

CONSTANTINOPLE   That feels . . . weird.

DOLORES   Momma?

CONSTANTINOPLE   Weird.

DOLORES   Mom.

CONSTANTINOPLE   OK.

DOLORES   Dear Mom, I am dead.

CONSTANTINOPLE   I want to see her.

DOLORES   Dear Mom, I am dead. I want to see you.

They contemplate.

CONSTANTINOPLE   Then what?

DOLORES   You sign it.

CONSTANTINOPLE   I can't write.

DOLORES   I'll just write your name and you can make
an X.

She does. He makes an X.

CONSTANTINOPLE   How does it sound all together?

DOLORES   Dear Mom, I am dead. I want to see you.
Constantinople. X.

CONSTANTINOPLE
(with pride)
My first letter.

DOLORES You did a good job. Except for the parts I wrote. Which are awesome.

CONSTANTINOPLE I came up with some of it.

DOLORES I'm a genius.

CONSTANTINOPLE I made suggestions. Like calling her Mom.

DOLORES I could deliver it.

CONSTANTINOPLE . . . You?

DOLORES Sure, me, why not me.

CONSTANTINOPLE I want to see her.

DOLORES I'll deliver it and tell you what she says and then you'll know if she wants to see you or not. Relax, chillaxe, kick back, you're four days old as of an hour ago. Enjoy the grandeur of a birthday weekend. Delegate responsibility. Yes?

CONSTANTINOPLE I don't know.

DOLORES That's a Yes.

DOLORES *gets up, gets ready to go out.*

CONSTANTINOPLE I want to come.

DOLORES Not yet.

CONSTANTINOPLE Why not?

DOLORES You're not old enough.

She leaves.
CONSTANTINOPLE *stands in the hotel room, fists clenched.*
He experiences being pissed off. He recognizes it.

CONSTANTINOPLE   Oh!
Wow.
I'm . . . "pissed off."
I want to . . . ARGGGHHH! And URGGGHHH! And—

He screams. It's a long drawn out wolf howl.
It's very intensely satisfying.
He kicks DOLORES'S *suitcase. Things fall out.*
He kicks it again.
He kicks clothes all over the room.
He throws things.
He wolf howls.
He jumps on the bed.
He stops, panting, out of breath.
He notices some of the clothes he's kicked around the room.
He likes them.
He puts them on. He dresses in DOLORES'S *dark, ripped, tight,*
sexy clothes.
He looks at himself and likes it.

CONSTANTINOPLE   I Am Constantinople.
I Am Four Days Old.
I Am Dead.
I Am Pissed Off.

Scene Eight

MORGAN'S *house. The basement.*
She and DOLORES *sit across from each other.*
The pumpkin sits in a baby bassinet.
DOLORES *is nervous, darting glances at* MORGAN *and around the room.*

MORGAN   The church of what, now?

DOLORES   The United Mormon Church of Mormons.

MORGAN   I've never heard of that. Is it new?

DOLORES   It's an off-shoot of an off-shoot. It's uh, an evolved form of our traditional beliefs.
Can I have a glass of water?

MORGAN   I thought you people didn't believe in evolution.

DOLORES   We don't, I'm speaking metaphorically. We believe in metaphors. Is anybody else at home?

MORGAN   I hate metaphors. I think things are what they are, or they're not.

DOLORES   I'm thirsty.

MORGAN   I'm an atheist.

DOLORES   You should think about God. Do you live
here alone?

MORGAN   You have brochures?

DOLORES   I forgot them in the car.

MORGAN   Look. You're not a Mormon. So what do
you want?

DOLORES   What makes you say that?

MORGAN   Mormons don't dress like that.

Beat.

DOLORES   We're the Reformed Mormon Church of
Mormons.

MORGAN   Yeah and I'm cheerful and well adjusted.
Seriously, who sent you? Did Elena send you?

DOLORES   Who's Elena?

MORGAN *stands in a heartbeat and twists* DOLORES'S *arm
behind her back.*
MORGAN *is very calm.*

MORGAN   Don't even think about fucking with me.

DOLORES   Lady, let me the fuck go, don't make me
hurt you.

MORGAN   *You* hurt *me?* I'll crush you like a graham
cracker.

DOLORES   I could kick your ass and not break a sweat.
So let. Go.

MORGAN *twists just a little harder.*
DOLORES *grits her teeth, macho.*

MORGAN   You tell Elena that I don't need any—
whatever you are—coming to my door with—whatever
you want.

DOLORES   I don't want to punch you after what you've
been through, but god help me I will.

MORGAN *releases* DOLORES.
They stare at each other.
DOLORES *is kind of excited and attracted.*
MORGAN *is sad.*

MORGAN   Elena told you.

DOLORES   I don't know any Elenas.

MORGAN   Then how did you know?

DOLORES   How did I know what?

MORGAN   What you said. "After what you've been
through."
Is it written all over my face?
You look at me and you see the aftermath of tragedy and
you feel bad?

DOLORES   No, not at all.
(beat)
I mean sort of, I guess, you don't look exactly sane and
normal, but whatever.

MORGAN   I lost a child.

DOLORES   I'm sorry.

MORGAN   There's a way women say that—"I'm sorry"—which is different from how men say it. Men get scared because they're afraid you're going to give them the details. Drop the V-bomb. They get vagina-terror and then they're not hearing a word, they're just waiting for the bomb to go off. But the women—the women get scared that tragedy is contagious, they'll go home and their kids will be dead. So now you know, you should go home. Keep your baby safely away from me.

DOLORES   I'm not pregnant.

MORGAN   No?

DOLORES   No.

MORGAN   You look pregnant.
(DOLORES *glances at her stomach*)
Not there. Not yet. In your eyes and your cheeks.

DOLORES   I do drugs. That's meth, not pregnancy.

MORGAN   You don't have meth-teeth.

DOLORES   Also, I have the flu, so I have a fever, so what you're seeing is a fever, not a baby.

MORGAN   It's cool if you're pregnant, I'm not gonna punch you in the stomach or anything.

DOLORES
(*it spills out*)

I'm going to kill it.
(half-beat)
So, you know, whatever.

Beat.

MORGAN   Sorry. About your arm.

DOLORES
(fast)
It's cool.

MORGAN   I. Sometimes I get. Overexcited.

DOLORES   No, don't sweat it, whatever.

MORGAN   My ex-husband thinks I'm—
(gestures: crazy)

DOLORES   You're not crazy.

MORGAN   No?

DOLORES   No, I don't think so, no.

MORGAN   I remember we watched *Jane Eyre* on HBO
once. When it got to the bit about the wife in the attic, he
made me turn it off. He said it struck too close to home.

DOLORES   I don't like movies like that.

MORGAN   Like what?

DOLORES   Ones where dumb bitches fall in love and
write in their diaries.

MORGAN *can't help it; she laughs, and is then surprised at herself.*

MORGAN
(trying to make up for laughing)
Watch your language in my basement. Please.
(beat—softer)
Are you really gonna kill it?

DOLORES   Why not?

MORGAN   I don't think Mormons believe in that.

DOLORES   I'm an atheist too.
(beat)
You're gonna tell me I shouldn't. Aren't you.
You're gonna say, "All life is precious."
But I don't think all life is precious. I don't even think most life is precious. So.

MORGAN   I wasn't going to say that.

DOLORES   No?

MORGAN   I think you're the only one who knows what you need to do. Like me. I was the only one who knew too.

DOLORES   You?

MORGAN   I'm forty-one years old. Everybody told me I was insane to have a child at my age. Withered. Ovaries like prunes, they said. But my body and I, we knew what we needed to do. Just like you do.
(beat)
Don't you?

A beat between them, intimate. Then DOLORES *shies away from the question.*

DOLORES You don't look that old.

MORGAN "That old." Wow. Well. I'm glad I seem less ancient than I am.

DOLORES I didn't mean it like that.

MORGAN You still didn't answer my question. Who you are. What you want. I mean, I haven't really left my basement in days, and from time to time I can hear the phone ringing upstairs and I feel like eventually somebody's going to call the police to see if I'm dead and decaying down here and that will be humiliating and inconvenient, all of which is to say I don't know why it matters who you are. I'm sort of beyond that kind of sanity. But still. I feel like I should have something to call you.

DOLORES Dolores. My name is Dolores.
Can I still have some water?

MORGAN That's a terrible name.

DOLORES No it's not.

MORGAN It means "Sorrows." Did you even know that?

DOLORES I don't think sorrow is terrible. Personally.

A beat between them.

MORGAN All right.

She goes to get DOLORES *a bottle of water from a box in the*
back. DOLORES *goes through the room fast, touching things,*
looking at them. She pockets some of the more expensive items.
MORGAN *returns.*

MORGAN   You're here for my husband, aren't you?

DOLORES   Your *husband?*

MORGAN   Ex-husband. It's all right, you're not the first
pretty little thing who's fallen hard. You can go stalk him
at his new apartment. His girlfriends will eventually find
his infidelity about as charming and original as I did.

DOLORES   I am not here for your husband.

MORGAN   He didn't know. About the child. I didn't
tell him. The day he came home and told me he was
leaving, I knew what he was going to say before he said
it. And I knew I was pregnant. And I just let him say
everything he'd practiced, and then I said, "Do what you
want." So he did.
(defensive)
What?

DOLORES   No, nothing, it's just—you don't look like
. . . you'd have had a *husband.*

MORGAN   What's *that* supposed to mean?

DOLORES   You look like the sort of woman who's got
better things to do than marry a man.

A beat between them. It is intense and kind of hot. MORGAN
looks away first.

MORGAN   I think you should go.

DOLORES   I came here for you. To talk to you.

MORGAN   I don't know you.

DOLORES   No not yet, but you could, you could
know me.

MORGAN   Give me one good reason not to ask you to
leave.

DOLORES   I have something you want.

MORGAN   I doubt it.
What?

DOLORES   Information.

MORGAN   You don't look like the kind of person who
has information.

DOLORES   I am the justice of the universe. I am a
universal messenger of peace and hope. God looked down
from the heavens and He said, "That lady is sad. That lady
has been treated unjustly." And in the interests of peace
and justice, He sent me. With information.

MORGAN   I would have picked someone else. What
information do you have?

DOLORES   Do you have anything stronger than water?

MORGAN   No. Dolores—if that is your name—

DOLORES   Beer? Whiskey? Vodka?

MORGAN   If you don't tell me—right now—what
you're talking about, I'll twist your arm again. I'll twist
it off. Also, you're too young to drink. And vodka is
disgusting, have some taste.

Beat. DOLORES *is intimidated, and likes her more for it.*

DOLORES   Here's the thing. It's classified information.
And I don't know how I feel about telling you this. But
there's someone who's—a great admirer of yours. A very
big—fan, I guess you could say.

MORGAN   Impossible.

DOLORES   I swear it.

MORGAN   I don't have fans. Let alone big ones.

DOLORES   *Huge.* An *enormous* fan.

MORGAN *is affected by this, even though she doesn't want to
show it.*

MORGAN   How do you know this—enormous—fan of
mine?

DOLORES   We met. By accident. This person spoke—
very highly—and at length about you. They want to meet
you.

MORGAN   So I don't know them.

DOLORES   You do and you don't.

MORGAN   They attended a lecture of mine. Maybe?

DOLORES   You give lectures?

MORGAN   I'm a professor.

DOLORES   A—seriously? A professor?

MORGAN   Your enormous person talked about me and
didn't tell you that?

DOLORES   You're too badass to be a professor.

MORGAN   I am *not*—
(it strikes her that this is a compliment; awkwardly:)
Thank you.
(beat)
A professor of entomology. Actually. Entomology isn't
badass. Unless it's like "vintage" and "retro" and whatever
you call it when uncool things are suddenly cool.
That's insects, by the way.

DOLORES   I know what entomology is.

MORGAN   You do?

DOLORES   I went to a private school. A boarding
school.

MORGAN   You don't look—

DOLORES   Like someone who went to a boarding
school?

MORGAN   How old are you?

DOLORES   I tried to hang myself twice. If you want to
know. In boarding school.

MORGAN   You—?

DOLORES   First from the light fixture. It broke. Then
from the bunk bed. It wasn't high enough. Then I quit.
Hanging myself and school, in that order. It's a long story.

MORGAN   That's terrible.

DOLORES   Why? Why is it terrible?

MORGAN   Because if you were my child, and I had not
given you a life that you wanted—that would be terrible.

This touches DOLORES, *and because it touches her, it makes her
mean.*

DOLORES
(getting up)
I'm not. I'm not your child.

MORGAN   Well I know that, but—.

DOLORES   I have to go.

MORGAN   Wait—Dolores. Wait.

A beat. DOLORES *studies her. Then:*

DOLORES   He was right. Your fan.

MORGAN   Right—?

DOLORES   You're not bad.

MORGAN   That's what he said about me?

DOLORES   I have to go.

MORGAN   Wait! Who—who is this person? And who are
you? And—

DOLORES   I really have to go. Things are just—you're
not what I—this is just not what I signed up for.

DOLORES *goes to the window. She shoves a chair under it, opens
it, and crawls out.*

MORGAN   Bye . . .

Scene Nine

The hotel. CONSTANTINOPLE *in* DOLORES'S *dominatrix clothes.*
He catwalks up and down the pool table.

CONSTANTINOPLE
(imitating DOLORES*)*
But only black though, that's the only color I have, I'm a
punk rock bitch, not a *girl.*

ELENA *walks in, wearing her carnival mask.*

ELENA   Dolores?

CONSTANTINOPLE
(startled)
Wow!

ELENA   You're not Dolores.

CONSTANTINOPLE   I am not Dolores.

ELENA   Do you work with Dolores?

CONSTANTINOPLE   I do work with Dolores.

ELENA   Oh, that's wonderful.
(takes off her mask)
I'm so glad we could reschedule.

CONSTANTINOPLE   But right now I'm "Pissed Off"
at Dolores.

ELENA   I imagine that happens often.
(pulls out a long roll of paper)
I brought a list with me of words that I find very upsetting.
Dolores was going to shout them at me, in no particular
order, I suppose. But if you find a particular order might
be more effective than another one, please don't restrain
yourself.

CONSTANTINOPLE *leans down from the pool table and takes the
list. He looks it over.*

CONSTANTINOPLE   What's this word?

ELENA   "Repugnant."

CONSTANTINOPLE   What does it mean?

ELENA   Disgusting. Vile. Causing . . . nausea. I cause
nausea.

CONSTANTINOPLE   Oh. What's this one?

ELENA   Putrid.

CONSTANTINOPLE   Shouldn't it be "PUH-trid?"

ELENA   No, the "p-u" is pronounced like Pyu. In this
case.

CONSTANTINOPLE   Oh. I'm only somewhat literate.
These are a lot of words. Are you sure you want me to say
all of them?

ELENA   That would be good, yeah.

CONSTANTINOPLE
(reading from the list)

Incompetent repugnant putrid—
(ELENA *is crying. He stops.*)
Don't do that. I'm sorry. I didn't mean it.

ELENA   No, this is good. Go on.

CONSTANTINOPLE   It doesn't look good.

ELENA   Please continue.

CONSTANTINOPLE   —murderous inhuman—

ELENA *is crying harder and louder.*

CONSTANTINOPLE   Can we not do this anymore?

ELENA   But there's more.

CONSTANTINOPLE   I don't like it when people do
that.

ELENA   Also, I may need you to beat me, but we haven't
gotten there yet. It's an option that Dolores suggested.

CONSTANTINOPLE   My mother won't stop crying and
it disorients me and makes my stomach upset and also I
can't find her, Dolores was supposed to find her but she's
not back yet and I think I'm more than Pissed Off, what's
more than Pissed Off? A word, I want a word for it.

ELENA   Angry.

CONSTANTINOPLE   I know that one and it isn't mean
enough.

ELENA   Furious.

CONSTANTINOPLE   It sounds limp.

ELENA   Livid.

CONSTANTINOPLE   Oh!
Wow.
Yes.

ELENA   Do you think you should beat me?

CONSTANTINOPLE   I don't know, I've never done
that before. Will you show me how?

ELENA   I thought you worked with Dolores. Shouldn't
you have done everything before?

CONSTANTINOPLE   I'm new.

ELENA   Can I borrow this?

*She takes the whip and clumsily brings it down on the pool
table.*

ELENA   You do it like that. I think? I don't know. I
watched some videos on the internet? It looked sort of like
that. All the women were thinner than me so I wondered
if this only works for anorexic women? But then at the
same time I keep thinking of the flagellants—they were
these radical monks in the Dark Ages and they beat
themselves and I think it made them feel better? About
life and suffering and guilt, primarily about guilt. So
maybe there's something to this after all. You're the
professional, what do you think?

CONSTANTINOPLE   Look I don't know, I don't
entirely understand when you talk, but all of what you said

sounds like . . . the opposite of wow. So maybe you should just tell me why you're crying.

ELENA   You're very different from other people.

CONSTANTINOPLE   I'm learning.

ELENA   I wanted to understand how this works. Punishment and purging. But there's something about it that just feels . . . unsatisfying. To me. I look at the meanness and it doesn't look like anyone is being truly punished and forgiven, it just looks like someone is being mean. But you. I've never seen someone so un-mean.

CONSTANTINOPLE   Is that bad?

ELENA   You could punish me in a way that I would *feel.*

CONSTANTINOPLE   Is that good?

ELENA   I think it could be wonderful.
(beat)
Have we met before?

CONSTANTINOPLE   I don't think so.

ELENA   You—there's something about you. It feels very familiar.

DOLORES *enters. She sees* ELENA *and stops.*

DOLORES   *You.* What are *you* doing here.

ELENA   Your assistant, Dolores. Is wonderful.

DOLORES *registers* CONSTANTINOPLE *in her clothes.*

DOLORES   What are you doing in my shit!

CONSTANTINOPLE   You're back!

DOLORES
(to ELENA)
Go away.

ELENA   But our appointment—

DOLORES   I said: get out.

ELENA   You're not going to help me. Are you.

DOLORES   I'm not here to *help* anyone, not him and
not you, I'm a delinquent dominatrix not Mother Teresa,
who the fuck do you two think I am! Get out!

ELENA *grabs her mask and stalks out.*

CONSTANTINOPLE   Did you find my mother?

DOLORES   Who said you could touch my shit?

CONSTANTINOPLE   Where is my mother!

DOLORES   I don't know.

CONSTANTINOPLE   You don't know?

DOLORES   I couldn't find her.

CONSTANTINOPLE   But you had an address.

DOLORES   She left town. For a while.

CONSTANTINOPLE *sits on the edge of the pool table. He puts his head in his hands.*

DOLORES   What are you doing?

CONSTANTINOPLE *starts to cry.*
He cries harder. He cries like ELENA.

DOLORES   What are you doing? Stop that. I hate when people do that. Come on, stop!
She'll probably come back.

CONSTANTINOPLE   When?

DOLORES   Soon probably.

CONSTANTINOPLE   Soon when?

DOLORES   Soon maybe next week—
(he cries harder)
Or this week—
(he cries harder)
Or tomorrow!
I'll re-deliver your letter when she comes back tomorrow.
Come on. Please?
Constantinople, *please.*

CONSTANTINOPLE *stops crying.*

CONSTANTINOPLE   I'll be even deader by then. I'll be stiffer. Look at me. My joints don't move as well. My fingers are getting blue. In a few more days I'll start to smell. If she doesn't like dead things, she'll not-like me even more if I smell.

DOLORES   I'll still like you.

CONSTANTINOPLE   You're not my mother.

DOLORES   But I like you. Even if you smell. So maybe
you should like me back.

CONSTANTINOPLE   I do like you.

DOLORES   You should like me more than other things.
You should like me most.

CONSTANTINOPLE   Shouldn't I like my mother
most?

DOLORES   You don't even know her. You know me.

CONSTANTINOPLE   I know her in a way I don't know
anyone. I know how she sleeps on her side and listens to
punk rock, her heart speeds up when there's punk rock on
the radio. And I know how much she likes pickles. She ate
pickles every day for the first four months. I got tired of
them after a while, so then she stopped, she said she could
tell I didn't like them. I don't know what she looks like
maybe, but the things I know about her, that's a kind of
knowing that weighs more than liking. Doesn't it?
(a beat, DOLORES turns away)
Dolores? Why does that make you sad?

DOLORES   I'm not sad.

CONSTANTINOPLE   You don't look happy.

DOLORES   I'm happy.

CONSTANTINOPLE
(gesturing to her stomach)
Maybe that's how she feels about you.

DOLORES   I don't think so.

CONSTANTINOPLE   Why not?

DOLORES   Because I don't want her. And she'd know that. So she'd hate me for not wanting her.

CONSTANTINOPLE   Maybe she doesn't hate you. Maybe it just makes her sad.

DOLORES   I don't want to talk about this anymore.

CONSTANTINOPLE   OK.

Beat.

DOLORES   We could write another letter to your mother. Where you tell her what you just told me.

CONSTANTINOPLE   And then she'll love me?

DOLORES   Yeah. Then she'll love you.

CONSTANTINOPLE   And then you'll find her?

DOLORES   Then I'll find her.

Scene Ten

Night in the basement. MORGAN *cradles the pumpkin and recites* Goodnight Moon *to it.*
She looks like she's showered. Her clothes are fresh.

MORGAN   Goodnight moon, goodnight bassoon, goodnight spittoon, goodnight little monsters and monsoons.

A stone bounces off the basement window.
MORGAN *stops and listens. It happens again.*
MORGAN *goes to the window, stands on a chair, and stretches up to shove it open.*
DOLORES *kneels down by the window.*

DOLORES   Hi.

MORGAN   I didn't think you'd come back.

DOLORES   Did you want me to?

MORGAN   What are you doing here?

DOLORES   I was accidentally coincidentally walking by and I saw the light in your basement was on. Can I come in?

MORGAN   I'm telling a bedtime story.

DOLORES   You could tell it to me.
Can I come in?

MORGAN   No.

DOLORES   How come?

MORGAN   You left last time. You didn't give me any
information whatsoever. You made me upset and then you
left.

DOLORES   I didn't make you upset. You were already
upset. You appeared less upset when I left.

MORGAN   I was not less upset, I was more upset
because a small girl had snuck into my basement,
pretended to be a Mormon, and then climbed out of my
window. That is why I was upset. You realize I could call
the police.
(pause)
Give me one good reason why I should let you in.

DOLORES   I was wandering through the world. And
everybody was boring. They looked the same, they walked
the same, they talked to each other in the same little
voices. And I thought: *Earthquake. Tsunami. Fire. Just
wipe them out.* I said that to God. And He said: *Hold on.*
And I said: *Just scrub the earth clean.* And He said: *Turn
around.* So I turned around. And there you were.

MORGAN   Me?

DOLORES   And you didn't stand like everybody else.
And you didn't move like them either. You certainly didn't
talk like them.

MORGAN   I'm not like everybody else.

DOLORES   And God said: *She's got something fucked up
and sad. She's got something real Real.*

MORGAN   I'm not fucked up.

DOLORES   And God said: *You still want a tsunami?*
Because you can have a tsunami.
But I said: *Hold off for a bit. I wanna see what her deal is.*

MORGAN   I'm fine. I'm fine.

DOLORES   No you're not. And you saved humanity
because of it.

A beat between them.

MORGAN   You're not dressed adequately.

DOLORES   I'm OK.

MORGAN   I don't know how anybody your age expects
to keep warm in that kind of get-up.

DOLORES
(shivering)
It's not that cold.

MORGAN   Oh for God's sake. You can come inside.

DOLORES *climbs through the window.*
An awkward beat between them.

MORGAN   Are you hungry?

DOLORES   Yeah.

MORGAN   OK. Look. Um. Stay here.

MORGAN *leaves and goes upstairs.*
When she's gone, DOLORES *takes the previously stolen*

knickknacks out of her pockets, puts them all back. MORGAN
reenters with a plate of casserole.

MORGAN (CONT'D)
All I have is casserole.

DOLORES   Did you make it?

MORGAN   No I did not make it. I do not make
casserole. I am not a person who makes casserole.

DOLORES
(devouring it with her fingers)
It's pretty good.

MORGAN   It's just leftovers.

DOLORES   It's awesome.

MORGAN   You should use a fork. You should be eating
better. You should be eating well-balanced meals. You
don't smoke, do you?

DOLORES   Of course I smoke.

MORGAN   Or drink?

DOLORES   Of course I drink! What's it to you?
(beat)
I'm going to kill it. I told you.

MORGAN   Why haven't you yet?

DOLORES   I'm sorry?

MORGAN   If you're so sure you want to kill it, then—
wouldn't you have already done it?

A beat.

DOLORES   You don't know what you're talking about.

MORGAN   Maybe not.

DOLORES
(furious, gets up)
You don't know what the fuck you're talking about. Look
at you!

MORGAN   Look at me?

DOLORES   You study insects. You have the fucking
luxury of studying insects. You have a pumpkin in a
bassinet. You got a real sweet life, and I'm glad, I'm glad
for you, because you wouldn't last a minute in mine. So
don't you dare think you're better than me.

Beat.

MORGAN   I was eighteen, the first time. Your age,
would be my guess. I wanted to go to college. I'd worked
so hard, I wasn't ready to give it all up. I got rid of that
baby. And you know what? Maybe one would think that
God is punishing me now. That this is the karma spilling
over all these decades later. But I don't think that. I think
that when I was eighteen, I did what I had to do. And I
think that now that I'm forty-one, I would have given
anything to be a mother. I don't think I'm better than
you. And I believe that nobody in the world has the right
to tell you what to do with your body. But if you knew
right now—the way I knew then—that you weren't going
to keep your baby, you would have already done what you
needed to do.

A long beat. The anger drains out of DOLORES. *She sits for a long beat. Then:*

DOLORES   How did it happen?

MORGAN   I'm sorry?

DOLORES   Your son. Who died.

MORGAN   Constantinople.

DOLORES   That's—a beautiful name.

MORGAN   You don't think it's strange?

DOLORES   Strange and beautiful.
Should I not ask? Is that impolite?

MORGAN   It's—no—
Yes—
It is, but—thank you.
It's nice. To be asked.
Nobody wants to hear this, you know.

DOLORES   I do.

MORGAN   It's easier for people when older children die.
Or fathers or sisters. But babies. How do you talk about
a baby? Nobody saw it. They imagined it, and it's just as
easy to un-imagine something. And it's bad taste, anyway,
to talk about dead babies.
Sometimes I think I'll strangle on the silence.

DOLORES   You don't have to be silent for me.

MORGAN   I'm of "advanced maternal age," that's what
they call it, but unlike you, I don't smoke and drink and—

whatever else you do. And I didn't want some high-tech slick C-section birth where they cut him out of me like a tumor. I wanted him to be—welcomed. Home. I wanted him to feel at home.

DOLORES   If I were gonna give birth, I'd want to be pumped so full of drugs that I don't wake up until the kid is sixteen and able to start working.

MORGAN   Or else you'd want to be awake and ready. Awake and listening. You'd have been waiting for nine months and you'd want every second of that arrival to be yours.

DOLORES   So you had him at home.

MORGAN   And everything was fine. And then all of a sudden everything wasn't fine. He came out still, so still. I waited for him to move, and he never moved. Never cried. His silence—was deafening. At night I still hear that silence ringing in my ears.
(beat)
She called 911 and they came but it was already over. They took him away so fast. I tell myself I didn't have a chance to hold his body—but I did—and I was scared of it—and then it was gone. And I'll never know—if it's just one of those things that turns so fast, too fast to be caught—or if he could have been saved. I won't know that. So it will always seem to me as if it was my fault.

DOLORES   You made the best decisions you could.

MORGAN   I should have made different decisions.

DOLORES   You made decisions.

MORGAN   That doesn't make me feel better.

DOLORES   I think it takes a lot of courage to make decisions. Even if terrible things happen afterward. It takes a lot of strength. You're a woman of strength. And I'd rather be strong than happy.

MORGAN   You're a child.

DOLORES   Maybe I'm not.

MORGAN   And the things you're saying—you don't understand yet what they mean.

DOLORES   Maybe I do.

MORGAN   I think you're more interesting than anything else I've seen in about forty-one years. But that doesn't mean we have anything to give each other.

DOLORES   I think we do though.

MORGAN   Why?

DOLORES   Because . . . you make me feel something else. In moments. Almost. Kind of. Like I could want to be . . . not-mean . . . to you. I've never felt like that before.

MORGAN   Dolores—

DOLORES   Have you?

MORGAN   Dolores—!

DOLORES   *Have* you?

MORGAN   No.

DOLORES   Until now?

MORGAN   I'm old enough to be your mother.

DOLORES   Let me. Just let me.

DOLORES *kisses* MORGAN. MORGAN *lets her, then breaks away gently.*

MORGAN   This isn't what you want. And it isn't what I want either.

DOLORES   I didn't even want to come here at first. And then I met you, and sure, you were sad, but you had an awesome house. You had nice things. I thought: *She doesn't even know how nice these things are. I'm sad too and I don't have any of that.* And the one thing I'd found that I liked—well, you were going to take that away too. You just didn't know it yet. And I went back to the motel I'm in this week, and I tried to dislike you, but instead I just thought about you. How all of your lines make angles I've never seen before. How your sad is brighter than other people's happy.

MORGAN   Dolores. Shhh.

DOLORES   Morgan, *please*—

MORGAN   Shh.

She puts her arms around DOLORES. *She holds her.*

DOLORES
(scared)
What are you doing.

MORGAN   Shhh.

DOLORES   Don't—I don't know what you're—don't
do that. Don't touch me like that.

But she doesn't pull away. MORGAN *holds her like you hold a
baby.*

MORGAN   We're adrift on a little boat. We're the only
two people on the face of the ocean. The apocalypse has
struck and land has become ash and the ash floats on the
water, and somehow, miraculously, we did not become
ash. We are the only things in the world that are more
substantial than ash. Just you and just me.
(DOLORES *starts to cry*)
Shhhh. Goodnight moon, goodnight bassoon, goodnight
spittoon, goodnight little monsters and monsoons. You're
doing your best. I can see that.

Scene Eleven

ELENA *sits under the pool table in the dilapidated hotel.*
She cradles a pumpkin in her arms.

ELENA   There there. Shhh. There's a good pumpkin.
(patting it)
Who's orange? Who's orange? Who doesn't rhyme with
anything?
(patting it)
Shhhh. What a good pumpkin you are.
This is how I brought you out. This is how I brought you
into the world. I didn't drop you. I never once dropped
you. You're so round.

CONSTANTINOPLE *enters.*

CONSTANTINOPLE   You're still here.

ELENA   I left but then I couldn't think where I would
go, so I came back.

CONSTANTINOPLE   Dolores is gone.

ELENA   I didn't come back for Dolores. I've given up
on Dolores.

CONSTANTINOPLE   She's been gone for one day and
one night and maybe I think I am giving up on Dolores
too.

(beat)
Why are you sitting under there?

ELENA   I just feel the need to be in a very small space right now.

CONSTANTINOPLE   Oh. Can I join you?

ELENA   That would make the space much smaller. So . . . I guess . . . yes.

CONSTANTINOPLE *crawls under the table too. A beat while he experiences the feeling.*

CONSTANTINOPLE   It's familiar.

ELENA   Yes?

CONSTANTINOPLE   But not dark enough. Not wet enough. Not warm enough.
This makes you feel better?

ELENA   It doesn't make you feel better?

CONSTANTINOPLE   I don't know. Not really. But maybe I don't know how to appreciate it. I haven't seen very much of the world after all.

ELENA   It's nice. The world is nice. But sometimes it's terrible.
(beat)
I lost my license.

CONSTANTINOPLE   What's a license?

ELENA   Something very important to me. A piece of paper.

CONSTANTINOPLE   Like a letter?

ELENA   Like a letter, yes.

CONSTANTINOPLE   What does it say?

ELENA   It says that I'm a good person. A useful person.

CONSTANTINOPLE   Why don't we write another one?
I'm good at letters.

ELENA   It's the sort of thing that can only be written
once.

CONSTANTINOPLE   Oh. That's very sad.

ELENA   I know.

CONSTANTINOPLE   So maybe you need a different
one.

ELENA   A different one?

CONSTANTINOPLE   A letter that says you are good in
a different way. Useful in a different way. Then it's not the
same one that can only be written once, it's a different one
that can only be written once.

ELENA *looks at him, taking him in.*

ELENA   Did you ever have your own ashram?

CONSTANTINOPLE   What's an ashram?

ELENA   Or maybe you taught yoga. Meditation. Before
this. I could see that.

CONSTANTINOPLE   You can?

ELENA   I can see you being a guru. A very successful
one with many followers.

CONSTANTINOPLE   What's a guru?

ELENA   What *is* a guru?
You're right. That's true.

CONSTANTINOPLE   It is?

ELENA   But then again, what *is* truth?
Why is one piece of paper truth? Or another piece of paper
truth?

CONSTANTINOPLE   You said it was.

ELENA   I did. I did say it was. But who dictates truth?
And are they gurus, is the hospital board made up of
gurus? I don't think so. What is an ashram? Why can't
this hotel lobby be an ashram? Why can't we all be truth-
seekers? Look at you. You're a dominatrix *and* you're a
truth-seeker.

CONSTANTINOPLE   I don't understand you again.

ELENA   I never thought about it that way at all. Thank
you. Really.

CONSTANTINOPLE
(*completely confused*)
You're welcome.

He looks at ELENA. *He likes her. He's sad.*
He turns away.

ELENA
(*studies him, surprised*)
What's wrong?

CONSTANTINOPLE   The thing is: this is wonderful.
You live in a world of wonderful things.
But it can't stay like this. I can feel things stiffening. It's
harder to move around. It's harder to be fast on my feet.
I have a daring and glamorous heart, but it is not beating.
And time is not on my side.

ELENA   Is that a Zen koan? Or a parable?

CONSTANTINOPLE   Dolores is gone again. And my
mother has stopped crying for the time being so I don't
know. I don't know. There are a lot of things I don't
know. And my heart that is not beating—it feels heavy.

ELENA   I'm sorry, I'm not good at parables. Tell me
again, and I'll try harder.

CONSTANTINOPLE *opens his mouth to reply—and then he hears
something. It changes everything. He jumps up from under
the pool table.*

CONSTANTINOPLE   Mom??
Mom!
Your heart is beating so fast.
It's almost louder than your crying.
I can hear you.
I can hear you.
And I'm coming.

CONSTANTINOPLE *takes off* DOLORES'S *dominatrix clothing.
He runs out.*

ELENA   Where are you going! Come back! Wait!
(looking at his discarded clothing—a realization)
Wait . . .
All this? For me?
(calling after him)
Thank you!

Scene Twelve

In the basement. MORGAN *and* DOLORES *are curled on the floor.* MORGAN *wakes up abruptly.*

MORGAN   I had the strangest dream.

DOLORES   Mmm.

MORGAN   Something was coming toward me. At great speed and velocity. A comet. A meteor. A freight train? Dolores, wake up.

DOLORES
(dreaming)
Do you want me to beat you or not?

MORGAN   Closer and closer and closer. Like a nightmare—but then it wasn't.
Because I wanted it. I was waiting for it.
(a sound at the basement window)
Dolores?
Did you hear something?
Dolores!

DOLORES
(sits up, disoriented)
What! Where! How much!

MORGAN   There's something at the window!

The basement window opens.
CONSTANTINOPLE *pokes his head through.*

CONSTANTINOPLE   Mom?

MORGAN   Oh God.

DOLORES   Oh my God.

CONSTANTINOPLE   I found you. I heard your heart
beating and I followed it and I found you. Mom?

MORGAN   Oh my God.

CONSTANTINOPLE
(seeing DOLORES*)*
You!!

DOLORES   You.

MORGAN   I know him. It's him. I know him.

CONSTANTINOPLE   Why can't she hear me?

MORGAN   His lips are moving but why can't I hear him!

CONSTANTINOPLE   Why didn't you tell me that you
found her?

MORGAN   He knows you. How does he know you?

CONSTANTINOPLE   Tell her it's me!

DOLORES   I'm sorry.

MORGAN   Dolores?

CONSTANTINOPLE   Dolores!!

MORGAN   What is going on!

CONSTANTINOPLE   Do something!

DOLORES   I don't know how to say this. So I'll just say
it. I know your son. He's wonderful. And he's dead, but
he still wants you to love him. And I wanted to help him,
and then I wanted to help you, but then I wanted you
both to love me, and I would have told you, eventually I
think I would have, but I'm sorry. I'm just. Sorry. And I
should go.

DOLORES *gathers up her dignity and slips out the window.*
MORGAN *and* CONSTANTINOPLE *are fixed on each other.*

CONSTANTINOPLE   Mom? I know I'm stiff.
And my hands are blue. And maybe I smell.
And I'm sorry. I'm sorry about those things.
But are you happy to see me? Even just a little?
Mom?

MORGAN   Constantinople.
I can't hear you but I know you. From the second I saw
you, I knew you.
You smell like my son.
You smell wonderful.

She reaches out to CONSTANTINOPLE.
She touches him.
It hurts her like nothing has hurt her before.
But it also feels right. Better than anything else has felt.
She wraps her arms around him.
She buries her nose in his neck.
She holds him.

MORGAN   Look at you.
Look at you.
I carried you. I sang to you. We liked the same songs. We
liked the same food. At first. But when you started liking
things that I didn't like, I liked that. I knew you were
going to be an individual. You were going to be strong.
You were going to be ornery. You were going to be the
kind of baby who jaywalks. I knew this about you. You
would have grown up an atheist, bilingual, bisexual,
bipartisan if I could help it. Maybe. Your favorite words
would be provocative ones. Look at you. Look at how
beautiful you are.

CONSTANTINOPLE   Mom.

MORGAN   You would have grown up to be somebody
I'd be proud of.
Whoever you would have grown into, I would have been
proud of you.

CONSTANTINOPLE   I'm getting stiffer. I'm getting
colder. You need to explain things to me. What happened.
Why I'm dead. I can't stay here much longer.

MORGAN   I dreamed about you. And in all the dreams
you were looking for me. And in all of them, you were
silent.

CONSTANTINOPLE   Mom, I don't understand
anything.

MORGAN   You broke my heart. You break my heart.
I didn't know I had a heart until you broke it.

CONSTANTINOPLE
(looking around the basement)

This is the record player. I heard this record player.
This is Tolstoy. You read me Tolstoy.
This is my house. It was. It was my house. You were my
house.
I don't recognize any of this anymore.

MORGAN   Please. Can you. Can we? Sign language?

CONSTANTINOPLE   Explain this to me. Explain. Tell
me why I'm dead.

MORGAN   I'll nurse you. Come here.

CONSTANTINOPLE   Did you not love me enough?
Did you not love me enough to keep me alive?

MORGAN   We can stay like this. I don't mind. I'll read
you your books. I'll take you for walks.
I'll make all the food you would have grown up to like.

CONSTANTINOPLE
(with quiet certainty)
You loved me. You loved me more than anything else in
the universe.
So it wasn't that.

MORGAN   I don't mind if we can't talk. Silence is
meditative. We can meditate.

CONSTANTINOPLE   I wanted to know.
I thought you could tell me and I wanted to know, why
I wasn't going to have all the things I wanted to have.
But you don't know either. So you can't explain.

MORGAN   We can't meditate, can we. This silence is
terrible.

You don't care about books or walks and you don't eat
food. You won't nurse.
You don't belong here, do you.

CONSTANTINOPLE   I wish you could.

MORGAN   I wish you did.

CONSTANTINOPLE   I wish you could make it all make
sense for me, because I like learning new things and I'm
very good at learning and that would be something I
would like to learn about. But I'm glad I found you. I'm
always going to be glad that I found you.

MORGAN
(*gathering herself*)
Mom will take care of this, Constantinople.
Mom understands, and Mom will take care of this for you.

Scene Thirteen

The hotel. ELENA, *dressed in the discarded dominatrix gear.*
There are pumpkins all over the pool table. ELENA *addresses*
them.
She is learning how to be mean, and it's exhilarating.

ELENA   The house rules, first-timers: If I get bored, I
stop. If I get tired, I stop. If you don't suffer in a manner
that I find enjoyable, I stop. And please, for the love of
God, don't talk about your feelings. Any questions?
(The pumpkins have no questions.)
Good. You vile orange lumps. Pestilent gourds. Putrid
misshapen squashes.

ELENA *puts nipple clamps on the pumpkin stems. She whips*
them gently. She breaks a sweat and stops for a breather.

ELENA   Mercy, you say? Mercy? We at Hotel Elena do
not believe in mercy. We here in the Dungeons Du Elena,
in the Palais Elena, in the Elenian Keep, we do not trade
in mercy. If you want mercy, go somewhere else.
*(*DOLORES *enters. She is sad and exhausted.)*
You're back!

DOLORES   What. Are you doing.

ELENA   Welcome to the Black Abyss of Elena. There's a
waiting list, but if you want to set up an appointment—

DOLORES   You're wearing my clothes.

ELENA   Your assistant is actually a guru and he gave them to me. Do you want them back?

DOLORES   No. I don't want them back.
I just want to be alone. In a very small space.

She curls up under the pool table.

ELENA   Uh . . . what are you doing? You can't lie there.

DOLORES   Just pretend I'm not here.

ELENA   I'm at work. I'm working. This is my new job and I'm good at it and I'm working.

DOLORES   I'm just going to fall asleep and a thousand years will pass and pumpkin vines will grow over my face and when I wake up, I won't remember anything. I won't remember a single thing from the life I had before. I'll be empty like an echo.

Beat. ELENA *puts the whip down.*

ELENA   Is everything all right?

DOLORES   No.

ELENA   Do you want to tell me about it?

DOLORES   No.

ELENA   Because you could, if you wanted. I wouldn't charge you.

Beat.

DOLORES   You look good.

ELENA   I feel good.

DOLORES   You never feel good. Why do you feel good?

ELENA   I was guilty and I was sad and I thought I
wanted to be forgiven. But then I realized that I don't
want that at all.

DOLORES   No?

ELENA   No. I want to be mean. I want to be
remorseless.

DOLORES   You don't seem very mean to me.

ELENA   I *wasn't*. I *wasn't* mean. But that was Old Elena.
Now I've cut through everything tying me to Old Elena
and I'm New Elena.

DOLORES   New Elena?

ELENA   New Elena is a happy person. New Elena is
incapable of moral conscience, and therefore is never
plagued by guilt. Your assistant suggested that course of
action.

DOLORES   He suggested that you become a dominatrix
incapable of moral conscience?

ELENA   I mean, he didn't spell it out, but he implied a
lot.

DOLORES   I don't think it works like that.

ELENA   Old Elena was a mess. Old Elena wanted to be
beaten. New Elena wants to beat.
Tell me that's not progress.

DOLORES   I don't know.

ELENA   You should try it too. You look miserable. You could use some progress.

DOLORES   I lied to someone.

ELENA   So become a person who lies.

DOLORES   I betrayed someone.

ELENA   So become a traitor. There's a long history of traitors, most of them are famous.

DOLORES   I'm a terrible human being.

ELENA   You're not.

DOLORES   Someone should do something terrible to me. I deserve it.

ELENA   That's not true.

DOLORES   I have a little person. I have something inside me that will grow into a little person, and I have no idea what to do with it.

ELENA   You don't have to know everything. You'll listen. It will tell you what to do with it. And even when you fail it, it will love you.

DOLORES   How do you know?

ELENA   Old Elena used to know a lot of things about that.

DOLORES   What if it looks at me and it sees someone it
doesn't like?

ELENA   You're very likable. If it makes you feel any
better. You're not the type of person I like very much, but
I like you.

DOLORES   You do?

ELENA   I do.

A beat. DOLORES *doesn't smile, but almost.*

DOLORES   Thanks.

ELENA   I know this isn't my job anymore, but—you
need to take care of yourself. Calcium supplements.
Vitamins. Are you seeing a medical specialist?

DOLORES   I thought you were a dominatrix incapable
of moral conscience.

ELENA   I'm just asking.

DOLORES   I don't know very much, I guess. And I fuck
up a lot. And you didn't ask me what I thought. But if you
want to know, I think the things you carry with you, the
things that are maybe the most important things—you
might try to put them down but you can't. If you woke up
in a hundred years, you'd still carry them with you. Maybe
over time your heart bends to fit the weight of those
things and that bending will turn you into a different
shape. But not a new shape. Just a different one. That's
what I think.

DOLORES *crawls out from under the table.*

ELENA   Where are you going?

DOLORES   I have to write a letter.

She leaves. ELENA *looks after her.*
Beat. The real world begins to filter back in.
ELENA *puts the whip down. She sighs.*

ELENA   My heart is a strange shape. A different shape.
But not a new one.
Not dominatrix-shape after all. I wish it were
dominatrix-shape.
It was good though. Wasn't it good?
While it lasted.
(a deep breath)
OK. I can do this. I'm going to do this.
Here I come.
I'm ready.

ELENA *walks back out into the world.*

Scene Fourteen

CONSTANTINOPLE *stands at the bottom of the basement stairs.*
He faces us.
Across from him, MORGAN *faces us.*
DOLORES, *now alone, sits holding her stomach.*
Sometimes their voices interweave in a choral effect.
Sometimes they don't.
Partway through, CONSTANTINOPLE *starts to move up the*
stairs. Stair by stair.

CONSTANTINOPLE   Dear Mom—

MORGAN   Dear Constantinople—

DOLORES   Hey kid.

CONSTANTINOPLE   I don't know how to write, so
I'm thinking you a letter, and maybe you'll understand.

MORGAN   I'm writing you a letter to take with you.

DOLORES   I'm bad at writing. Or talking. Or feelings.
But here it is.

CONSTANTINOPLE   You're . . . wow.
And this was . . . wow.
And there were moments that were just . . . really . . .
wow.

MORGAN   You're beautiful.

And this was beautiful.
And I've never been so sad in my life.

DOLORES   You're the only other person in the world
who's ever lived inside my skin.
We might understand each other better than anyone else
on the planet.
Even if I don't think I know what to do with you.

CONSTANTINOPLE   Parts of it sucked too. But I
thought it was beautiful.

MORGAN   I don't know what happens after this. I wish
you were finding out with me.

DOLORES   So I'm waiting for you. Wide-eyed. Awake.
For your arrival.

CONSTANTINOPLE   I wanted to see what I'd miss.
I'm glad I saw. But it isn't mine after all.

MORGAN   I'm glad I held you. I was afraid to do it, and
I did it, and it was wonderful after all.
And I will always love you no matter how dead you are.

DOLORES   I might love other people in my lifetime.
But not like this.

CONSTANTINOPLE   Maybe next time. If there's a next
time. Maybe I'll try it again. I don't know.

MORGAN   I'll miss you.

CONSTANTINOPLE   I'll miss you.

MORGAN   I'll miss you.

DOLORES   Whenever you want to come out . . . I'll be
here.

*A beat—*CONSTANTINOPLE *is on the last stair.*

CONSTANTINOPLE   Thank you.

*He steps backward into the dark. And is gone. The light fades
on* DOLORES.
MORGAN *is alone.*
*A beat—listening—waiting—*MORGAN *reaches and finds that
great thread of sorrow. It will always be there now.*

MORGAN   Time will pass and I'll grow older and
beautiful things will come to me.
The leaves will fall and winter will come and winter will
melt and spring will come and spring will explode into
summer which comes like a hot breath and then it will
cool into autumn. And this will happen, it will happen, it
will happen again and again, and every time it will be
beautiful. I will get older and my hair will become silver
and the lines around my eyes will deepen and perhaps that
too will be beautiful. The pain will stay the same, and I
will get stronger and I will find, in that strength, a certain
beauty. I will hope for other children, not to replace you,
but to share you with them—the love I have for you, that
will spill over onto them, that is beautiful. This will be my
life, and perhaps—it seems to me—it will be beautiful. And
the saddest thing in the world is not sharing it with you.
And I will miss you
And I will miss you
And I miss you . . . still.

Lights down on MORGAN *standing alone.*

End of play.

Acknowledgments

Still owes a great deal to Lisa Heineman, who shared with me her experiences of love, motherhood, and grieving in the months after her son, affectionately nicknamed Thor, was stillborn. To Lisa, her partner Glenn Ehrstine, and to Thor, all I can say is: Wow.

Deep thanks to Alan MacVey, Sherry Kramer, and Marsha Norman for their mentorship and guidance of this particular play and of me as a playwright. *Still* would not exist in this form without Alan and Sherry's thoughtful dramaturgical engagement and Marsha's enthusiastic support. My thanks also to the MacDowell Colony, the University of Iowa Playwrights Workshop, Loyce Arthur, and the multiple companies and collaborators who have workshopped this play along the way, in Iowa, New York, DC, and North Carolina.

Finally, a special thank-you to Mom, Dad, and Chris for everything, absolutely everything.